NELSON ROLIHLAHLA MANDELA

A Great Leader who could change South Africa

THE HISTORY HOUR

※

"During my lifetime, I have dedicated my life to this struggle of the African people. I have fought against white domination, and I have fought against black domination.

I have cherished the ideal of a democratic and free society in which all persons will live together in harmony and with equal opportunities. It is an ideal for which I hope to live for and to see realized. But, My Lord, if it needs to be, it is an ideal for which I am prepared to die."

※

The final lines of Mandela's 60-page, 176-minute statement when he stood in the dock in the Palace of Justice in Pretoria, South Africa, on the morning of April 20, 1964 - nearly half a century before his death December 5 at the age of 95.

CONTENTS

❧ I ❧
INTRODUCTION

❀❀❀

Did you know that 28% of Africa is made up of wilderness? Now, compare that to the fact that 38% of North America is wilderness.

❀❀❀

Think about that for a moment.

❀❀❀

A lot of people in North America have the perception that Africa is mainly wild with elephants, giraffes, and other wildlife roaming about. Meanwhile, many who haven't been to North America might get the perception that it's comprised of a lot of cities since large cities such as Los

Angeles, Toronto, Chicago, and New York are all in North America.

৩১৫৩

North America has more wilderness than Africa. Sometimes, it's a little shocking to realize that your perception of something is wrong. It makes you start wondering what other ideas and opinion you have might also be wrong.

৩১৫৩

Like what you may have heard or read about Nelson Mandela. Thus, this begs the question: "*who is Nelson Rolihlahla Mandela?*" If you're like a lot of people all over the world, you've probably wondered who he is and perhaps why he has a larger-than-life legacy.

৩১৫৩

Maybe you've ever wondered about the lessons to be drawn from his life stories. The truth is, there's a lot of contradictory and even outright false information floating around about this great man.

৩১৫৩

That's why we rolled up our sleeves and uncovered all the latest information and lessons to be learned from the man famously known as *'Madiba.'*

৩১৫৩

And what we discovered is that apart from his towering

legacy, he was also flawed like any other human being or politician.

⚜

Surprised?

⚜

Then you'll be even more surprised when you discover:

⚜

- The top 3 decisions that made Nelson Mandela a great leader
- Ten ways Nelson Mandela changed the world
- How Nelson Mandela inspired the world
- The top 5 ways Mandela transformed South Africa
- How Nelson Mandela became an inspiration for the aged - a case study of Elizabeth Marie Mkame
- How Nelson Mandela showed courage
- Seven leadership qualities exemplified by Nelson Mandela
- The best three books about Nelson Mandela

So, without further introduction, let's jump in with a discussion of *"**The Top 3 Decisions That Made Mandela A Great Leader...**"*

✲ II ✲

DECISIONS COOLER THAN MICHAEL JORDAN - THE TOP 3 DECISIONS THAT MADE NELSON MANDELA A GREAT LEADER

"It always seems impossible until it's done."

— NELSON MANDELA

✦

The life story of Nelson Mandela has become a legend that cuts across all culture, language, race or border. Indeed, the world needs his leadership lessons.

✦

His decades of imprisonment and the apartheid issues he faced cannot be compared in any way to the problems faced by any business leader. But, if you aspire to be a great leader, you need to embrace the key lessons from Mandela's decisions at some points in his career.

ॐ

For me, here are the top three of such decisions:

REFUSING CONDITIONAL
AMNESTY OFFERED BY BOTHA
IN 1985

৩১৬৪

P ro-apartheid president F. W. Botha offered Mandela freedom in his speech in 1985 to the nation but on the condition that he has to renounce violence and any other '*illegal*' activity.

৩১৬৪

He aimed to blame Mandela himself for remaining in prison - at least, he has given him the choice of freedom provided he is ready to obey the law.

৩১৬৪

But Mandela was not deceived by this clear deceit even though he has been confined to a small cell with decades of hard labor.

৩১৬৪

For Mandela, he believed this would go against ANC's long struggle, his leadership, and his principles.

৩৯৩

Here is an excerpt of his reply to the then president:

৩৯৩

> *"What freedom am I being offered while the organization of the people remains banned?... What freedom am I being offered if I must ask permission to live in an urban area?... Only free men can negotiate. Prisoners cannot enter into contracts."*

৩৯৩

Mandela refused the offer from Botha; instead, he remained in his cold, dark prison cell, preferring to serve the remainder of his life president.

৩৯৩

By the way, the size of his cell was 8 feet by 8 feet.

৩৯৩

Since this vital decision considerably elevated his position as the face of the ANC's opposition, it was a compelling decision.

৩৯৩

Also, it also showed that he doesn't mind sacrificing his personal life to achieve his goal.

MAKING PEACE IN 1993 WHEN
CHRIS HANI WAS ASSASSINATED

૭✲ૐ

This second vital decision was made almost immediately when Mandela was a free man in 1993, but it was before he was made president (he was made president in 1994).

૭✲ૐ

When Chris Hani was stepping out of his car, he was shot in cold blood by a white extremist. Chris Hani was a famous black leader who was also fighting for equal rights.

૭✲ૐ

The killer was turned in by a white woman who had identified him. After the assassination of Hani, there was widespread fury and a lot of demonstrations.

૭✲ૐ

While many blacks desired revenge, it would have been the perfect setting for mayhem, violence, and looting.

⚜

But Mandela appealed for calm despite just being out of prison.

⚜

Here's an excerpt from his statement:

⚜

> *"Tonight, I am reaching out to every single South African, black and white, from the very depths of my being. A white man, full of prejudice and hate, came to our country and committed a deed so foul that our whole nation now teeters on the brink of disaster.*
>
> *A white woman of Afrikaner origin risked her life so that we may know and bring justice to this assassin. The cold-blooded murder of Chris Hani has sent shock waves throughout the country and the world. Now is the time for all South Africans to stand together against those who, from any quarter wish to destroy what Chris Hani gave his life for - the freedom of all of us."*

TURNING DOWN THE CHANCE TO BECOME PRESIDENT FOR A SECOND SUCCESSIVE TIME IN 1994

☙❧

T his third vital decision was made almost immediately after he became the elected president.

☙❧

He decided that he won't stand for a second term in office early in his first term. In a continent where leaders tend to seek maximum power (Robert Mugabe comes to mind!), this was such a noble act.

☙❧

Mandela knew that more than a billion people would be watching his speech all over the world; hence, he wanted to prove his allegiance to the true democracy.

☙❧

Also, he wanted to show the citizens of his country that he was for them regardless of the color of their skin.

❦

The stone in Robben island contains a part of the most famous lines of this remarkable speech.

❦

Here's an excerpt from the speech:

❦

> "At last, we have achieved our political
> emancipation, and we are fully committed to
> liberating ourselves from any form of
> discrimination such as poverty, suffering, gender
> problems, and deprivation.
> This beautiful land shall never, never and never
> again experience the oppression of one by
> another..."

❦

A strong focus on the future, not the past, power-sharing, forgiveness without forgetting, and racial harmony were the greatest attributes, which Mandela's extraordinary achievement sought to encourage.

❦

Through his magnanimity towards his former enemies,

Mandela supported his strategy and proved to be a master of symbolism.

⊙⧉⊙

For instance, he visited the widow of prime minister, Hendrik Verwoerd, in 1995. Hendrik Verwoerd was the major proponent of the apartheid regime which was one of the reasons why Mandela was imprisoned.

⊙⧉⊙

Also, despite being fully aware that the national rugby team (the Springboks) has been a symbol of racism and Afrikaner power for decades, he jubilated when they won the world championship. During the championship match, he proudly wore the team's shirt and waved his hands in support.

⊙⧉⊙

Through these acts, he showed the world that he was in complete support of having a rainbow nation.

⊙⧉⊙

These leadership traits exhibited by Mandela are few and far between.

❧ III ❧

CHANGES THAT ARE SCARIER THAN TYRA BANKS - 10 WAYS NELSON MANDELA CHANGED THE WORLD

"Education is the most powerful weapon which you can use to change the world."

— NELSON MANDELA

❦

The name Nelson Mandela is synonymous with strength and strong conviction.

❦

But no simple statement can show the different ways this fearless leader changed politics both around the world in his home country - South Africa.

‧❀‧

As a summary of the adaptation of Mandela's autobiography - long walk to freedom - which he wrote when he was in prison, here are ten ways Nelson Mandela changed the world: (by the way, the adaptation was produced by Justin Chadwick, while Idris Elba played the role of Nelson Mandela.)

THE IMPORTANCE OF ENGAGING
YOUTH IN THE POLITICAL
PROCESS

꧁꧂

O ne of Mandela's key projects was to firmly establish the youth league of the African national congress (popularly known as the ANCYL) after he joined them in 1994.

꧁꧂

Mandela co-opted his longtime friend Oliver Tambo to work with him in achieving his vision since both of them understood the importance of political awareness.

꧁꧂

Bear in mind that in 1940, Mandela and Tambo took part in a protest against the policies of the University of fort hare and were both expelled.

ENGAGING IN NON-VIOLENT PROTESTS TO SHOW THEIR GRIEVANCES

༄༅༆

In 1948, the national party became the country's governing party. Then, it introduced a system of racial segregation (popularly known as apartheid) which allowed the white minority majorly to be in the position of authority.

༄༅༆

Immediately, the ANC and the ANCYL organized several peaceful acts of civil disobedience such as series of boycotts and peaceful protests.

༄༅༆

Mandela headed the 1952 campaign for the defiance of unjust laws in 1952; volunteers had to travel all over the country to get involved in the peaceful protests against the discriminatory practices of the national party. The only ammunition they had were some freedom songs and a strong desire for equal rights.

⚜

In the same year, the first black law firm in the country was opened by Mandela and Tambo; citizens who had been affected by the apartheid were offered low-cost and pro bono legal services.

⚜

Despite their peaceful actions, over 150 activists including Mandela were arrested in 1956.

⚜

Their charges?

> *"High treason and a countrywide conspiracy to use*
> *violence to overthrow the present government*
> *and replace it with a communist state."*

⚜

However, they were all acquitted of this charge four years later.

STEADFASTNESS IN ONE'S CONVICTIONS

ॐ

During what became known as the Rivonia trial, Mandela could have easily used various legal loopholes to help his case since he was a skilled lawyer.

ॐ

Instead, he was truthful in admitting his wrongs and held on firmly to his beliefs.

ॐ

Though Mandela was firm in his belief that his actions were justified in the fight for equal rights, he didn't avoid dealing with the consequences of the wrongs he had committed.

ॐ

Mandela explained to the court the purpose of his fight during his opening statement.

⚜

Part of which was an equal place in the society, the decimation of the national curfew, land ownership rights and a living wage for all Africans.

⚜

Here are excerpts:

> "I have dedicated myself to this struggle of the
> African people during my lifetime. I have fought
> against both white and black domination. I have
> cherished the ideal of a democratic and free
> society in which all persons live together in
> harmony and with equal opportunities.
> It is an ideal which I hope to live for and to achieve.
> But if need be, it is an ideal for which I am
> willing to die."

REMAINING COMMITTED TO
ONE'S POLITICAL ETHICS
REGARDLESS OF THE SITUATION

⬥

During the Rivonia trial, Mandela only escaped the death sentence by whiskers but was sentenced to life imprisonment.

⬥

He would serve the first 18 years of the 27 years he served in Robben Island prison - a former colony of lepers.

⬥

The color of his skin was a testament to the fact that he would receive harsher treatment than his fellow inmates. For one, his tiny cell had no plumbing and no bed.

⬥

Also, he could only be visited by his wife Winnie twice within the year. While these conditions might break some men, Mandela endured.

☙❧

In fact, he would go ahead to earn a degree in law from the prestigious University of London. He also educated other inmates on how to resolve conflicts without using violent methods.

☙❧

It was in these conditions that he wrote and smuggled out his autobiography titled "*long walk to freedom,*" and after five years of his release, this autobiography was published.

☙❧

Even if only symbolically, he was able to maintain his position as a leader in the fight against apartheid through the political statements he continued writing.

☙❧

Through the "*free Nelson Mandela*" campaign organized by Oliver Tambo in 1980, the international community became alert to the institutional racism that existed in South Africa and the plight of Nelson Mandela. This campaign created more pressure on the South African government.

☙❧

Hence, when the pressure was too much, the government

gave him political conditions for his release, one of which was for him not to be involved in any violent political action.

۞

Mandela rejected the offer.

۞

He was moved to a mainland prison and a minimum security correctional facility in 1982 and 1988 respectively. But newly elected president F. W. De Klerk ordered the release of Mandela from prison on February 11, 1990. He said he wanted a non-apartheid South Africa.

CORRECTING PAST MISTAKES
ONCE AND FOR ALL

❧

T o ensure that no political activist suffered the same fate as he had, Mandela went to work almost immediately after his release from prison.

❧

Mandela who represented the ANC worked with the national party to end apartheid in South Africa once and for all. Through this achievement, both the de Klerk and Mandela earned a Nobel peace prize award in 1993.

❧

The first-ever multiracial elections in the country took place on April 26, 1994, with over 20 million South Africans showing up to take part, and the ANC was voted in as the governing body.

❁❦❁

Thus, Mandela became South Africa's first black president on May 10, 1994. The establishment of a truth and reconciliation commission was among the first tasks on his agenda.

❁❦❁

The role of this commission was to investigate many political and human rights violations that have happened in the country since 1960.

CREATING A GENUINE
MULTIRACIAL GOVERNMENT

❦

A part from fulfilling his promise of political emancipation which he made during his inauguration speech, Mandela wanted to develop an actual multiracial government to ease fears of the white population in the country who were under the rule of a black majority for the first time.

❦

Hence, Mandela and his cabinet guaranteed equal unqualified citizenship rights to all South Africans after spending two years to draft a new constitution for South Africa.

❦

In his autobiography, Mandela wrote of the constitution,

"the apartheid regime had put law and order in disrepute. Due to this crude practice and through my personal beliefs, I exploited all the avenues to enhance respect for the judiciary, law, and order."

INSPIRING CHANGE AT A
GLOBAL LEVEL

❧

B eing an inspiration for a global scale change is one of the hallmarks of any great politician.

❧

Mandela continued to spread his message of equality around the world even after stepping down as president in 1999.

❧

For instance, he served as a mediator during the Lockerbie case between Great Britain and Libya.

❧

For his efforts towards racial equality, Mandela was celebrated around the world both at home and abroad, he was decorated with more than 250 international honors, one of which was the presidential medal of freedom by George w. Bush in 2002.

REMAINING A FORCE TO BE RECKONED WITH - DESPITE HIS RETIREMENT

❀❀❀

Mandela was still actively involved in meetings, appearances, and consultations despite giving up his role for a quieter life in 1999.

At the age of 85 (in 2004), he announced that he genuinely wanted to retire and he told the press,

"I will call you, don't call me."

Yet, the work of the organizations that he reorganized and founded still echoed his voice. Through strategic partnerships, educational opportunities and the promotion of social justice in all parts of the world, the Nelson Mandela foundation continues to work tirelessly to maintain the values promoted by Mandela.

They are involved in many causes such as the fight against poverty, development of rural and under-utilized land, health-care improvement, and finding the solution to HIV/AIDS.

PRESERVING YOUR DIGNITY

❧

While it is unarguable that the most significant legacy by Nelson Mandela was the destruction of apartheid in South Africa, the dignity he maintained throughout is life, and many political ordeals were one of his most significant contributions to humanity.

❧

Bear in mind that his battle for equal rights was not quickly and he had to spend more than a quarter of his life in prison, he never allowed the challenges in his personal life to corrupt his vision for equal rights. He had to go through a divorce; he had difficulties with his health and even his battle with the law which was the most obvious challenge.

❧

Mandela will always be remembered for putting the good of his people before his comfort and not allowing the cruelty experienced during his time in prison shape the path of his future.

IV

CAN KIM KARDASHIAN INSPIRE THE WORLD? HOW NELSON MANDELA INSPIRED THE WORLD

"A good head and a good heart are always a formidable combination."

— NELSON MANDELA

Through his exemplary life and talent, Nelson Mandela has left a legacy that can hardly be rivaled all over the world.

Part of such legacy were the words he spoke which are usually a source of inspiration especially when we are having challenges in different aspects of our lives.

Apart from being one of the greatest leaders of the world, his life has shown us what it truly means to be an advocate of freedom.

❧

Nelson Mandela's words.

❧

When you read his writings, it would seem as if you are having a face to face conversation with him.

❧

He had the gift of expressing himself in the exact way he wanted on paper.

❧

Most of the quotes shared below were excerpts from the time when he was in prison.

SOME OF HIS MEMORABLE QUOTES ABOUT DEATH AND MANKIND

❦

"If I had time over, I would do the same again, so would nay who dare calls himself a man."

❦

"if I have to die, I declare for all who want to know that I will go to meet my destiny."

❦

"Death is something inevitable. When a man has done what he considers to be his duty to his people and his country, he can rest in peace. I believe I have made that effort and that is, therefore, why I will sleep for eternity."

SOME OF HIS MEMORABLE QUOTES ABOUT HIS PRINCIPLES

❧

"...poverty is not natural, it is human-made, and it can be overcome and eradicated by the actions of human beings. Overcoming charity is not a task of charity, it is an act of justice."

❧

"We need to make the eradication of poverty one of the top priorities in the world and understand that we all share the same humanity; diversity is our greatest strength."

❧

"The anchor of all my dreams is the collective wisdom of mankind as a whole."

❧

"The action of the masses can overthrow governments."

"We find ourselves at the dawn of the African century, a century in which Africa will occupy its rightful place among the nations of the world."

"If the development of the African nation had not been interrupted by the white settlers, the same thing would have happened as in Europe, but without having contact with them."

"Education is the most powerful weapon which you can use to change the world; education is the great engine of personal development. It is through education that the daughter of a peasant can become a doctor, the son of a mineworker can become the head of the mine, that a child of farmworkers can become the president of a great nation."

SOME OF HIS MEMORABLE QUOTES ABOUT LIFE

❦

"Until it's done, it always seems impossible."

❦

"The greatest glory in living lies not in never falling, but rising each time we fall."

❦

"Do not judge me by my successes, judge me by how many times I fell and got back up again."

❦

"There is nothing like returning to a place that remains unchanged to find ways in which you have altered."

❦

"Friends with independent minds allow you to see problems from all angles, and I like them."

❦

"If you want to speak to a man's head, talk to him in the language he understands. But if you want to speak to a man's heart, talk to him in his own language."

❦

"The foundation of spiritual life for any soul are the qualities which are within reach of such souls. They are honesty, sincerity, simplicity, readiness to serve others, absence of vanity, and pure generosity."

❦

"Forgiveness removes fear; it liberates the soul."

❦

"I learned that courage is not the absence of fear, but the triumph over it. The brave man is he who does not feel afraid, but he who conquers that fear."

❦

"What matters in life is the difference we have made

*in the life of others and not the mere fact that we
have lived."*

᪥

I am sure one or more of these quotes would have inspired you in one way or another just as it has inspired me even as I am typing this.

᪥

Hence, I suggest you write down and keep these with you wherever you go.

V

MAKING CHANGES TO BE A BETTER LOVER - THE TOP 5 WAYS MANDELA CHANGED SOUTH AFRICA

"I learned that courage was not the absence of fear, but the triumph over it. The brave man is not he who does not feel afraid, but he who conquers that fear."

— NELSON MANDELA

The eradication of apartheid remains the most significant legacy of Nelson Mandela even though it has been almost two decades since there has been an end to this legalized racial discrimination in South Africa. Those who are aged 18 or under won't have experienced the discrimination of blacks by whites backed by law, but this has been truly happening since the colonial times when races were separated.

Until Mandela's release from prison in 1990, which allowed him to start negotiations with the president at that time - Fredrik Willem de Klerk, South Africa continued to enforce racial division, denying the black population the right to vote. When multi-racial elections were held for the first time in 1994, it signaled the end of the apartheid.

৩৵৶

After being released from prison in 1990, Mandela's African national congress continued with its struggle against apartheid by remaining committed to their armed conflict.

৩৵৶

Even when it seemed that the country was heading for a racial bloodbath after the 1993 assassination of ANC arrowhead Chris Hani by white extremists; Mandela issued an appeal:

> *"this is the time for all South Africans to remain united in fighting those who from any part of the country wish to demolish what Chris Hani gave his life for - the freedom of all of us."*

৩৵৶

Apart from the eradication of apartheid, here are four other ways Mandela changed South Africa:

PEACE AND FORGIVENESS

❧❧❧

Despite spending 27 years as a political prisoner, Mandela's personal determination that anger over past crimes shouldn't motivate future laws and actions was one of his most significant influence on the new South Africa.

❧❧❧

He laid a firm foundation for this by establishing a truth and reconciliation commission in 1995. This commission was tasked with the responsibility of investigating the violations of human rights in the history of the country and taking appropriate measures to end it.

HERALDING THE COUNTRY'S RE-ENTRY INTO THE WORLD STAGE

꧁꧂

Mandela heralded the country's re-entry into the world stage through his inauguration speech in 1994 where he said, the country should never again be seen as the "***skunk of the world***" but should become a "***rainbow nation.***"

꧁꧂

He said:

> *"we enter into a covenant that we shall build a society where both black and white South Africans can walk tall without being afraid but they are sure that they have the right to human dignity, which cannot be forfeited - a rainbow nation at peace with itself and the world."*

ESTABLISHING A NEW
POLITICAL PATHWAY

۞

When South Africa formally transitioned into a democracy, blacks were allowed into polling booths and the corridors of power.

۞

Thus, South Africa lost its status of being a castaway from the global community.

۞

Recall that there had been sanctions against apartheid from most countries all over the world, most notably, the united states They placed a trade embargo and a ban on direct flights to South Africa.

RENUNCIATION OF VIOLENCE

◈

One of the defining moments of the political process was forsaking bloodshed. This renunciation of violence earned de Klerk and Mandela the Nobel prize for peace in 1993.

VI

HOW NELSON MANDELA BECAME AN INSPIRATION FOR THE AGED - A CASE STUDY OF ELIZABETH MARIE MKAME

"After climbing a great hill, one only finds that there are many more hills to climb."

— NELSON MANDELA

৩৯৩

Elizabeth Marie Mkame is an active board member for help-age affiliate - the Muthande society for the aged.

৩৯৩

One of the top reasons why he became an inspiration for Elizabeth was his decision to step down as president after just one term because he believed other capable hands could run the country.

🕉️

One key lesson for Elizabeth here is that leadership should not be hoarded.

🕉️

Here are three other vital lessons Elizabeth learned from Nelson Mandela:

DEVELOPING SOUTH AFRICA IN A WAY THAT CAN BE SUSTAINED

❦

Since Mandela made decisions that can help South Africa to attain sustainable development, Elizabeth became more involved with her community.

❦

Her work aims to inspire others, when she's reminded by the people she has helped, she always feels encouraged to do more.

❦

When she worked with the Diakonia council of churches, the church buildings were used to establish 14 community resource centers for the training of young people.

❦

Most older people who were unable to access the benefits of their spouses after the death of their spouses because they couldn't pay lawyer's fees were the biggest beneficiaries of these centers.

⚜

Despite the hard work, she remained patient in showing love and respect to those in need.

⚜

Through the work of these centers, Elizabeth got the idea that there is dire need for an organization that caters to the needs of older people.

MAKING THE VOICES OF OLDER
PEOPLE HEARD

❧

S ince people were being forced to move from one area to another, Elizabeth was moved to be involved in the setup and building of a home for the aged. Nelson Mandela gave many people the hope that one day they would be free even though the dismantling of their family structures was incredibly disheartening for them.

❧

Today, the rights and entitlements of older people in South Africa are secured and are protected by the constitution. Despite the challenges in the implementation, older people were still able to make their voices heard through campaigns such as age demands action. This could only have been achieved because of Mandela's leadership.

❧

Since it was the culture of Mandela to see progress as quickly as possible, he encouraged many businesses to build schools and clinics in all parts of the country especially the rural areas. He affirmed that everyone living in the country is also part and parcel of the country.

PUSHING THE RIGHTS OF OLDER PEOPLE

❦

Since one of the desires of Nelson Mandela was peace and stability in the world, Elizabeth has been inspired to travel long distances with the '*Age Demands Action group*' to encourage and inspire young and older people to help and understand one another in creating a better environment for all and sundry.

❧ VII ❧

COURAGE IS THE NEW BLACK - HOW NELSON MANDELA SHOWED COURAGE

"Money won't create success, the freedom to make it will."

— NELSON MANDELA

※

The embodiment of magnanimity and reconciliation as depicted by Mandela is yet to be seen or acknowledged in the history of mankind. He personified the spirit of *Ubuntu* setting aside repression, subjugation, decades of colonial division, and enduring 27 years in apartheid prisons.

※

He firmly believed that for individuals and society to prosper, people have to depend on one another. He wanted the prosperity and peace not just in South Africa but also in Bosnia, Rwanda, Columbia, Israel, Palestine and all other parts of the world.

⚜

Though Mandela pointed out that the many accolades that are accorded to him should also be accorded to the people that surrounded him who were loyal, more youthful, and even brighter than him, this wasn't entirely true.

⚜

The truth is, his compassion and capacity to empathize with others deepened during the 27 years he spent in prison.

⚜

In addition to being exposed to leadership and culture while growing up, and being a voice for young people in their quest to end apartheid politics, he seemed to have developed a better understanding of the human condition while in prison.

⚜

The Mandela who came out of prison was almost flawless just like a precious diamond perfected from the deep ends of the earth. He preached the message of forgiveness and reconciliation rather than call for his pound of flesh. This message of forgiveness and reconciliation and many other extraordinary noble acts became an inspiration for young and old people.

⚜

An example of being an embodiment of what he proclaimed was inviting his former jailer as a VIP guest to attend his presidential inauguration. He invited him to lunch at the presidency, the man who led the state's case against him and called for the imposition of the death penalty at the Rivonia trial. Also, he visited Betsy Verwoerd in the enclave of Orania, Betsy was the widow of the high priest of apartheid, and the enclave of Orania is a white Afrikaner-only enclave.

۞

Though he displayed a few insecurities attributed to most politicians, Mandela was sufficiently comfortable in his abilities to differentiate the good from the bad.

۞

He accepted criticism and was quick to apologize when the need arises. He was courageous enough to oppose the official policy of his beloved ANC both in actions and in words when he didn't agree with their opinions and actions.

۞

Mandela had the grace to publicly accept the report of the truth and reconciliation commission (TRC) when they published their findings, despite the fact the ANC strongly opposed the release. At a time when the South African government was uncertain in their response to the HIV/AIDS pandemic, Mandela through his foundation established the first rural aids treatment site in South Africa.

۞

As president, Mandela appointed a judicial commission to investigate the involvement of a TRC commissioner who was accused in an amnesty hearing. Mandela also had his weaknesses. His steadfast loyalty to his organization and his colleagues was one of his main weaknesses.

⚜

He allowed incompetent and grossly underperforming members of his cabinet to remain their position rather than have them dismissed.

⚜

More about his weakness or weaknesses in a later chapter. Even after his retirement, his passion for serving drove him to continue his long walk.

⚜

As the government that succeeded his government seem to have faltered in the face of the HIV/AIDS epidemic, Mandela continued to campaign vigorously for those affected by the disease. Also, he continued to raise funds for children and for other projects that can serve the best interest of others.

⚜

His courage showed in the transparency of his character until his death.

❧ VIII ❧

THE MACGYVER OF LEADERSHIP - 7 LEADERSHIP QUALITIES EXEMPLIFIED BY NELSON MANDELA

"There is no passion to be found playing small - in settling for a life that is less than the one you are capable of living."

— NELSON MANDELA

❦

Nelson Mandela was a man who gave so much for his people and is arguably the most famous man to have come from Africa.

❦

Even the harshest of his critics will agree that he demonstrated the attributes of an extraordinary man.

⚜

This begs the following questions:

- What made him unique from other political leaders around the world?
- Many of his colleagues, some who may have even achieved more are now in the history books, why is Nelson Mandela immortalized?

⚜

After some extensive studies about him, here are the top seven reasons why he was an outstanding leader:

WILLINGNESS TO SACRIFICE
HIMSELF

❧

During the 27 years he spent in prison, he was made to hammer rocks during the day in the scorching heat and retire to a tiny eight by seven concrete cell that had only a straw mat for him to sleep.

❧

In 1985, when he refused "*freedom*" and said,

> *"your freedom and mine cannot be separated! When I and you, the people are not yet free, I cannot and will not give any undertaking."*

DISPLAY OF LOVE

❦

G ranted it might be easier to forgive a stranger and perhaps a friend, how about an enemy? But Nelson Mandela forgave the apartheid government - his greatest adversary.

❦

He chose the higher route rather than demanding for the head of those thousands of innocent South African black indigenes. Mandela left a lasting legacy of forgiveness and reconciliation for the world and his people when he set up the truth and reconciliation commission.

LOVER OF LEARNING

part from exercising on a daily basis while in prison, he also read as much smuggled books as he could.

He was not permitted to read political books (which would have been his preference), but as a lover of learning, he read books on gardening and horticulture.

Thus, he was able to cultivate the foods for his fellow prisoners and the prison officials.

Also, he continued to educate himself about the legal profession and gave legal advice not just to fellow prisoners but also to prison officials.

❦

Due to his quest for learning and teaching, Robben island was renamed as the "***Nelson Mandela University.***"

PUTTING PEOPLE AND HONOR
BEFORE WORLDLY GAIN

৩৯৩

These days, people are not interested in how you acquire money, power, and wealth; they are just interested in the money, power, and wealth.

৩৯৩

But the reverse was the case with Mandela. He put honor and people before worldly gain. When he was president, Mandela's estate was around $2.9 million compared to most other African presidents who were accumulating fortunes corruptly during their tenures.

UNITING PEOPLE OF ALL RACES

※

R emember the adage, "***divided we fall, united we stand.***" When Mandela was elected president, one of his first significant roles was to unite the whites and the blacks. In truth, most people expected him to give more privileges to blacks than whites, especially those from his tribe (the Xhosa tribe), but he didn't.

※

Currently, South Africa is enjoying the benefits of rich diversity in economy, intellect, and culture. In the words of F. W. De Klerk, the last president of the apartheid era, Nelson Mandela was a *"great unifier with an outstanding lack of bitterness."*

FOCUSING ON THE NEEDS OF OTHERS BEFORE HIS OWN

༺☧༻

He listened to those ignored or labeled as castaway by the society. He was a servant to people of all levels, the poor, the rich, the educated and the illiterate.

༺☧༻

He never saw any enemy; everyone was his brother and sister. While he was busy empowering his people, most rulers from other parts of the world were busy empowering themselves and their friends.

SHOWCASING HIS WEAKNESS AS A HUMAN

৩৯৩

Though the media classified him as an infallible saint to the whole world even to Africans, Mandela himself acknowledged his weaknesses. He was unable to balance being a leader in the home with being a leader of the nation; he had two failed marriages. Also, he failed to raise children that befitted his noble status.

৩৯৩

He once said in an interview:

> *"My first task when I came out was to destroy the myth that I was more than an ordinary human being."*

While this may be disappointing, lots of people were still drawn to him. Perhaps, his admission of being human appealed to more people.

❧ IX ❧
THE NELSON MANDELA'S GUIDE TO LEADERSHIP LESSONS - TOP 7 LEADERSHIP LESSONS TO LEARN FROM NELSON MANDELA

"No country can really develop unless its citizens are educated."

— NELSON MANDELA

❧

While December 5th of every year will always be a day to remember Nelson Mandela, the heroism he displayed while alive will continue to live forever in the hearts of many especially South Africans.

❧

While his countrymen would always celebrate him, I realized

one common theme in all of his pictures that I have seen - he is always full of smiles. This would be my first lesson from this fearless leader.

❧

Apart from the smile, you will discover six other leadership lessons to learn from Nelson Mandela in this chapter.

❧

SMILE

❧

Your ability to smile, laugh and find joy in just being alive shouldn't be taken away by external circumstances.

❧

Most times, we allow things beyond our control to have significant impact on lives such that we lose our joy.

❧

Mandela walked out of jail smiling and waving to half a million supporters despite spending 27 years in prison under harsh conditions, conditions which could have broken anyone.

❧

Having found a new lease of life, he continued to smile and share his unconditional love and humor with everyone.

❧

The truth is, if we all learn to smile and laugh more, this world would be a better place. In the words of Mandela,

> *"laugh hysterically, but breathe peacefully and tread softly."*

SHOW LOVE TO YOUR ENEMIES AND WHEN NECESSARY, WORK WITH THEM.

❧

Mandela made efforts to work with his enemies for the good of the country even when he knew he might lose the support of his people. He acknowledged that collective action (even with people who had once oppressed him) was key to the development and progress of the country.

❧

In his words,

> *"you have to work with your enemy to make peace with your enemy. Then, you become his partner."*

Most times, we are quick to oppose both in actions and words, the people who don't believe in our ideals.

❧

Hence, you need to determine whether or not it is required to work with your enemies to improve the lives of others. If there is a need to work with them, figure out common ground and start rebuilding from there.

❧

BITTERNESS AND HATRED IS THE GREATEST PRISON

❧

Here is how Mandela puts it,

> *"as I walked out the door towards the gate that would lead to my freedom, I knew that if I didn't leave my bitterness and hatred behind, I'd still be in prison."*

Most of us hold on to bitterness and hence, are living in our own self-imposed prisons which poisons both our spirits and our surroundings.

❧

Until you let go of past hurts (real or imagined), you cannot indeed have peace. Mandela also said,

> *"resentment is similar to drinking poison and hope your enemies will be killed."*

LEARNING CONTINUES REGARDLESS OF YOUR AGE

۞

Mandela earned his law degree through a correspondence program from the University of London at the age of 70 and while in prison. He firmly believed that the most powerful weapon to change the world is education.

۞

You can pursue a degree. Learn a new language, become a better-informed citizen by actively seeking out knowledge and you can learn anything you desire. Always remember, you can learn anything no matter your age.

۞

YOUR PURPOSE SHOULD BE TO SERVE OTHERS

۞

Right before he was sentenced to life imprisonment, Mandela made a rousing speech, which though was meant to be censored came out to the world nonetheless,

> *"I have dedicated myself to this struggle of the*
> *African people during my lifetime.*
> *I have fought against both white and black*
> *domination; I loved the idea of a free society in a*

democratic setting in which all persons are at
peace with one another and have equal rights.
While I hope to live and achieve it, if necessary, I am
prepared to die for it."

❧

Through his works and words on earth, Mandela kept showing that our purpose is to serve others first and leave a lasting legacy for future generations.

ALLOW DIFFICULTIES TO MAKE YOU AND NOT BREAK YOU

❧

The many challenges we encounter in life can quickly make us lose vision or distract us from the initial plans we had for our lives.

❧

Mandela's fellow prisoners established the fact that Mandela was a man of vision who remain determined, and kind. He was even a leader for them in the face of harsh conditions. He refused to compromise his ideals for the easy way out when he had the opportunity to gain his freedom by giving up his pursuit to end apartheid.

❧

When he was released from prison, he said,

*"if you have the iron will and the necessary skill,
there are few misfortunes in this world that you
cannot turn into a personal triumph."*

❧

These words should be a part of our watchword.

BELIEVE YOUR DREAMS WILL EVENTUALLY COME TO REALITY

❧

Mandela dedicated himself to the vision of a free South Africa because he believed his vision would eventually become a reality. So much was his belief that the rest of the world also believed in him.

❧

This vision led to the growth of the anti-apartheid movement, which also consisted of individual efforts who believed in the vision. All great leaders realize one thing, the obstacles of accomplishing a goal is always less important than achieving the goal itself.

❧

Do you have any dream you so much believed that you are willing to put everything you have into it?

❧

By living out the rest of our own lives applying Nelson Mandela's universal ideals, we would be paying him with the highest tribute. Let me end this chapter with another quote from this great man:

☙❧

*"There is no passion to be found in settling for a life
that is less than the one you are capable of living."*

ꙩ X ꙩ

IS REMEMBRANCE PHONY? HOW TO REMEMBER NELSON MANDELA EVERY WEEK

"Courageous people do not fear forgiving, for the sake of peace."

— NELSON MANDELA

ꙩꙩ

The commemoration of the life and struggles of a remarkable man can be done in so many ways. Launched by the UN and inspired by Nelson Mandela himself, July 18 is now known as Nelson Mandela international day.

ꙩꙩ

Here are ten ways to remember this man on a weekly basis:

BE ACTIVE AND KNOWN FOR SOMETHING

❧

According to the Nelson Mandela Foundation, the idea behind the day is to encourage and enable individuals to have a positive impact on others every day. It follows the attributes of Nelson Mandela who became an inspiration for positive global movement.

❧

The motto of the foundation is: take action, inspire change and make every day Mandela day. Mandela gave up 67 years of his life in the pursuit of social justice.

❧

Hence, the foundation is imploring every person, groups and even companies to spend at least 67 minutes of every July 18 (every other day when they can) to give back to the society. Walks, converts, acts of service and other events are always used to mark that event all over the world.

BE AN AGENT OF GROWTH

❧

Apart from the actions of service which many South Africans will perform to commemorate Mandela day, a group is remembering that day by encouraging people to plant and maintain their vegetable gardens.

To achieve this goal, Dis-Chem foundation, Johannesburg city parks and Zoo, African children's feeding scheme and citizenship initiative lead formed a partnership together.

VISIT HIS MONUMENTS

Both in and outside South Africa, there are monuments of Nelson Mandela that you can visit. For example, the Nelson Mandela sculpture in Howick KwaZulu-natal created by Marco Cianfanelli to mark the anniversary of the day when the police captured Mandela.

SHARE YOUR FAVORITE MANDELA QUOTE

For those who preferred a digital way to mark the day in 2014, the un and the Mandela foundation allowed such people to upload a 30 second audio or video of them singing or reading any of Mandela's quotes and stories that may have inspired them.

From these uploads, an official video was released and promoted on YouTube.

CELEBRATE WITH DANCE

❦

As part of the events to celebrate the 2014 edition in Glasgow Scotland, Hugh Masekela (South African Trumpeter) headlined the concert.

❦

Svend Brown, the director of music at Glasgow life said,

> *"by bringing together musicians from Scotland and South Africa, we are thrilled to honor him on Glasgow. We have the Mzansi youth choir (dubbed the voices of the youth and the future), and the legendary Hugh Masekela. We can only hope the great man loved what we've done."*

MEET UP

❦

There are many places of worship all over the world where the day is always marked with services. For example, in one of the editions, the Riverside Church in New York held a musical tribute titled, "***the footsteps of Mandela.***"

ASSIST OTHER NOBLE ORGANIZATIONS

❦

Bikers for Mandela day ride partnered with support organizations to help survivors of gender-based violence and rape.

TIDY UP THE ENVIRONMENT

❦

If you are a South African and you are in Washington dc, you can liaise with the South African embassy to work with NGOs especially Martha's table.

❦

This NGO is involved in various humanitarian services such as organizing a community thrift store, preparing food for the mobile soup kitchen, and tidying up education classrooms.

WATCH A FILM

❦

I suggest you watch the movie "***Mandela: long walk to freedom.***" This movie was released in 2013 and remains the highest grossing movie in the history of South African film.

WALK DOWN MANDELA STREET

❦

If you live in Britain, this is very easy because there are over 25 roads named after Mandela. But the Mandela street in

Camden, North London has the closest link to Mandela - it was the headquarters of the international anti-apartheid movement in the 1980s.

❧❧❧

The ten ideas shared above are just that - ideas. You can come up with your unique way of celebrating the day.

❦ XI ❧
WHAT YOU COULD LEARN FROM NELSON MANDELA'S JOURNEY TO BECOMING PRESIDENT

"It is better to lead from behind and to put others in front, especially when you celebrate victory when nice things occur. You take the front line when there is danger. Then people will appreciate your leadership."

— NELSON MANDELA

❦

While the primary focus of this chapter is Mandela's journey to become president, you will also discover some of the events that happened when he was president and after he retired from active politics.

❦

Oliver Tambo (a friend and colleague to Nelson Mandela) was

elected as the ANC's national chairperson, while Nelson Mandela himself was elected as the president of the African national congress (ANC).

⚜

To achieve the first non-racial elections in the country, negotiations between the then president - F. W. De Klerk and Nelson Mandela continued.

⚜

The first convention for a free South Africa was first held on December 21, 1991, at the world trade center in Johannesburg.

⚜

Though many black South Africans wanted a complete transfer of power, the white South Africans were only willing to share power. This led to tense negotiations and eruption of violence across South African townships as demonstrations were taking place unabated.

⚜

In the midst of these demonstrations and being under pressure, Mandela was still able to balance the political weight with the intense negotiations. After the successful negotiations between the black and South Africans, the first multi-racial democratic elections took place on 27 April 1994.

⚜

Here is a breakdown of the votes:

- ANC - 62.65 percent. They emerged as the winners
- National party - 20.39 percent
- Inkatha freedom party - 10.54 percent
- Freedom front - 2.2 percent
- Democratic party - 1.7 percent
- Pan Africanist Congress (PAC) - 1.2 percent
- African Christian democratic party - 0.5 percent

❀❀❀

On 10th of May 1994 and at the age of 77, Nelson Mandela took his oath of office as the first black president in the history of South Africa, while F. W. De Klerk became his first deputy.

❀❀❀

Despite having the majority of the votes, the ANC formed the government of national unity, which was headed by Nelson Mandela.

❀❀❀

Unknown to many, Nelson Mandela secretly wrote his autobiography, which he titled "*long walk to freedom,*" while in prison, he launched this autobiography in 1994.

❀❀❀

Apart from his published autobiography, he also authored and co-authored many other books such as "***Nelson Mandela's*** *favorite African folktales,*" "**Nelson Mandela: the struggle is my life,**" and "**no easy walk to freedom.**"

⚜

Note: all these books are available on Amazon; I encourage you to read them all.

⚜

Just go to '**Amazon.com,**' input Nelson Mandela into the search box and hit enter, all these books will be displayed.

⚜

You can then click on each of them to make your purchase.

⚜

For bringing South Africa back into international football, FIFA awarded him the order of merit in 1995.

⚜

Apart from working hard to prevent the collapse of South Africa's economy when he was president, he also had to solve the issues created by the '**almost twenty years**' of apartheid rule in the country. The top three among such matters were unequal access to social services, inequalities, and poverty.

⚜

A socio-economic policy framework called the reconstruction and development program (RDP) which was implemented by the ANC government of Nelson Mandela was introduced in 1994.

❧❦❧

This was introduced to address most of the problems caused by the apartheid regime with particular emphasis on poverty alleviation and proffering solutions to the lack of social services across South Africa.

❧❦❧

Through this policy, the government was able to provide jobs, primary health care, and housing.

❧❦❧

In his effort to promote peace, nation-building, and reconciliation between the black and white South Africans, Mandela used sports as a significant focal point. He encouraged the blacks to support the national rugby team who were hated at that time because all the team members were white.

❧❦❧

A new constitution was signed into law by Mandela in 1996, the primary aims of this law were in two-fold:

❧❦❧

- To guarantee the rights of the minorities and the freedom of expression
- To establish a stable central government based on majority rule

❖❖❖

On December 4, 1996, the constitutional court approved the constitution of the Republic of South Africa, while the law took effect on 4th February 1997.

❖❖❖

A macroeconomic policy called the growth, employment, and redistribution (gear) was introduced in June 1996. The primary goal of this policy was to achieve a rapid liberalization of the South African economy.

❖❖❖

In 1998, the South African government under Nelson Mandela announced its intention to buy a twenty-eight BAE/SAAB JAS 39 Gripen-fighter aircraft from Sweden at a total cost of 10.875 billion Rands (which translates to $65 million or 388 million Rands per place).

❖❖❖

This purchase was made to modernize the defense equipment of South Africa's department of defense. Subsequently, the arms deal, as it was later known, was accused of gross embezzlement of funds. Despite sitting president Jacob Zuma's inquiry into this case of corruption in 2011, no headway is yet to be made.

❖❖❖

Though Mandela retired from active politics in 1999, he still served as a mediator in brokering peace agreements in

Burundi - a central African country. With the support of the regional peace initiative (RPI), the Arusha agreement for peace and reconciliation was signed on 28 August 2000.

❧❧

These peace processes established the signing of two cease-fire agreements:

❧❧

- The transitional government of Burundi (TGOB) and the Burundi armed political parties and movements (APPMS) signed the first of these agreements on seven October, 2002.
- The TGOB and Pierre Nkurunziza's CNDD-FDD signed the second of these agreements on December 2, 2002

❧❧

In South Africa, Nelson Mandela's children funds were used to help settlements of poor people particularly their schools and classrooms. One of the ways Mandela raised funds for this initiative was to invite business leaders to accompany him on his visit to the settlements of the poor and have them pledge donations there.

❧❧

The facilities provided by this initiative are now known as the "***Madiba magic.***"

❧ XII ☙

MANDELA'S WEAKNESSES - THE BIGGEST BLUNDERS BY NELSON MANDELA

"As long as poverty, injustice and gross inequality persist in our world, none of us can truly rest."

— NELSON MANDELA

❧❧❧

It is arguable that Mandela's retreat from public life happened at the exact time when the high ideals of the liberation movement collapsed into the lowest state of corruption under Zuma.

❧❧❧

It may even be further argued that had he been active in the last few years before his death, he would have held president Jacob Zuma accountable for his actions the same way he held his successor, Thabo Mbeki, accountable over Mbeki's aids-denialism.

⚜

But the truth is, the rot had begun when Mandela was still president.

⚜

An example would be the famed multi-billion dollar arms procurement deal that eventually became the poisoned well of politics in South Africa.

⚜

Mandela is often misunderstood because he has had to live with the burden of being a living saint.

Through his political career, he wasn't a saint, but he was immensely creative.

⚜

Also, his perceived sainthood has had some adverse effect on the growth of democracy that he fought for so hard to establish.

⚜

It can be argued that Mandela's passion for being an HIV/AIDS activist was based on the fact that his government didn't respond adequately to the epidemic when he was president.

Hence, he sought to make amends.

Since much of the economic infrastructure that kept the minority South Africans in power was still intact, the white corporate world cheered when he was released and when he became the first black president of South Africa.

Also, when Mandela accepted an international monetary fund's plan, it handed over the resources of the country and the services to private companies.

When he was president in 1997, he chose to give his country's highest award for a foreigner to Colonel Muammar Gaddafi (Libya's dictator) because he donated $10 million to the ANC.

Also, the corrupt Indonesian president, Suharto, was given the same award because he donated $60 million.

Since he didn't make any public statement to stop the hanging of Ken Saro-Wiwa, he showed his support for Sani Abacha.

❦

His children had also talked about how he was not present in their lives as a father when he was in prison and even when he was released because most of his time after his release were spent on political and public duty.

❦

After divorcing his second wife Winnie Mandela in 1996, he has had two failed marriages.

❦

While he apparently has his flaws like any other human, his endurance and strength in overcoming the enemies of peace and cooperation should be an inspiration to all.

BOOKS AS FIERCE AS RUPAUL - THE BEST THREE BOOKS ABOUT NELSON MANDELA

෯෯

In the opinion, here are the best three books about Nelson Mandela that I have read:

Long Walk To Freedom: The Autobiography Of Nelson Mandela by Nelson Mandela

෯෯

Conversations With Myself by Nelson Mandela and Barack Obama

෯෯

Mandela's Way: Lessons For An Uncertain Age by Richard Stengel and Nelson Mandela

❦

BONUS:

❦

Who was Nelson Mandela? By Pam Pollack and HQ

❦

You can find all of these books on Amazon, and I encourage you to read them all.

✣ XIV ✣

DEATH, OUR WEAKEST LINK - HOW NELSON MANDELA DIED

"There can be no keener revelation of a society's soul than the way in which it treats its children."

— NELSON MANDELA

༺༒༻

Before his death, he was hospitalized for more than a month. The severity of the situation was demonstrated to South Africans and the global community when his family, his second wife, Winnie Mandela, and other close friends were seen visiting him immediately after he was admitted.

༺༒༻

There were conflicting media reports that circulated the

media throughout his stay in the hospital. While some would say he was stable, some would say he was unresponsive.

⚜

The revered icon was still alive to celebrate his 95th birthday, and his birthday coincided with the internally-celebrated Mandela day. The Philippines, Bolivia, and cities like Rome held community service to commemorate the day. After his death, there was a brief family feud regarding his burial preparations.

⚜

Nelson Mandela, the son of Chief Henry Mandela of the Temby tribe, was born in Transkei, South Africa on July 18, 1918.

⚜

Having enrolled at the university college of fort hare, he became the first member of his family to attend school. He would later seek to become a qualified lawyer after enrolling from the University of Witwatersrand in 1942.

⚜

From 1944, Mandela devoted his energies to non-violent struggle against the country's apartheid regime for almost two decades. Though he was eventually acquitted, his struggles earned him a treason charge.

⚜

When this wasn't yielding the results he desired, he began to advocate for armed struggle in 1961. Hence, he established the youth league of the ANC called Umkhonto We Sizwe.

He was tried twice and eventually sentenced to prison after he organized a 3-day workers' strike. After battling with a recurring lung infection, Nelson Mandela died at the age of 95. Mandela left behind his wife Graca Machel, three daughters (Zindzi, Zenani, and Makaziwe), four step-children, seventeen grandchildren, and eleven great-grandchildren.

❦ XV ❧

CELEBRATING CENTENARIES CAN BE SEXY - CELEBRATING THE CENTENARY OF NELSON MANDELA'S LIFE

"Forget the past."

— NELSON MANDELA

❦

To have a proper understanding of Nelson Mandela, we have to understand his life as a complex human who changed through the course of his life.

❦

If we break the ritualistic references of empty phrases such as him being an "*icon,*" only then can we truly learn from him.

Celebrating the anniversary of Nelson Mandela's life presents us with the opportunity to meditate on the character of his life.

One significant part of that character is his leadership prowess, a freedom fighter that acts in the present but has the future in mind.

This makes him ready to advance the cause of freedom regardless of the conditions which may be significantly different from the one experienced at that time.

Hence, to assess what may have changed or caused the change, there has to be an analysis of the forces at work.

Though this requires firmness on principles, there has to be flexibility in executing the policies.

This type of leadership is often lonely because it is not easy.

Most of the editorials and blog posts celebrating the life of Nelson Mandela will be stating the obvious fact - the cause of his fight is justified.

❦

So, they use platitudes and other adjectives to state this obvious fact and accord him with the title of an "*icon.*"

❦

The truth is, we have to grapple with the often controversial problems and complexities in his life before we can have a full understanding of a leader like Nelson Mandela.

❦

Compared to the range of legacies that we need to interrogate, only one reference is made to Mandela's legacy.

❦

Many aspects of Mandela's life can be scrutinized; they include his ethics, leadership principles and value, violence and non-violence, questions of legality, and politics concerning gender.

❦

If you check a book published by the HSRC in 2006, there is only one reference to the "*meaning of Mandela.*"

❦

This presents more problem than having a single interpretation of his legacies. The reason is that we are only affirming the fact that the life of Nelson Mandela has no controversy, thus, should not be debated.

๑๑๑

If you take a careful and ample examination of his life, you will discover a multifaceted human being with a lot of complexities.

๑๑๑

At various stages of his life, the conditions in the presence of Nelson Mandela changed. Thus, he also adapted as a human being.

๑๑๑

Mandela himself expresses the changes in his journey through life by the titles he gave his books:

๑๑๑

- No easy walk to freedom (a derivation from Jawaharlal Nehru)
- Long walk to freedom and most recently,
- Dare not linger (a posthumous publication by Mandla Langa, Macmillan, London, 2017)

๑๑๑

One other problem with the book, "***the meaning of Mandela***" can be found in the dedication which reads thus;

꧁꧂

"To Nelson Rolihlahla Mandela - for the gift of freedom."

꧁꧂

This preface presents various problems in understanding the real "***meaning***" or meanings of Mandela.

꧁꧂

First, Mandela did not believe that only one action or one day led to his freedom.

꧁꧂

This belief is one of the reasons why his most recent book "***dare not linger***" refers to the arrival at a location - a milestone in achieving freedom, but with more walks and journeys required.

꧁꧂

Thus, he gave this quote from the book "***long walk to freedom***" in the new book:

꧁꧂

> *"I have walked that long road to freedom. I have tried not to falter: I have made missteps along the way. But I have discovered the secret after climbing a great hill; one only finds out that there are many more hills to climb...I can rest only for a moment, for with freedom come responsibilities*

and I dare not linger, for my long walk is not
yet ended."

In each of his works, Mandela indicates that the struggle for freedom is a continuous journey.

❧

Despite his larger-than-life status, not even Mandela would have claimed or said that he was solely responsible for the freedom given to his people - this is another problem in this dedication.

❧

There are many people and many, many struggles that led to the freedom which Mandela achieved in his later life.

❧

His release (and that of other political prisoners) from prison was secured and democratic elections ultimately attained through the efforts of those who died, suffered, and sacrificed in many ways, including Mandela himself.

❧

Mandela was present was not present in all of the struggles during his lifetime, but he played a central role in many of these struggles.

❧

He had the support, action, and power of many other men

and women who were involved in advancing the cause of freedom.

࿐

However, Mandela soon realized that more work was needed to be done to deepen and broaden the quality of the freedom achieved after being sworn into power in 1994.

࿐

Now that you have a better understanding of the complexities that surround the life of Nelson Mandela and the various interpretations that can be derived from these complexities, here are three highly appreciable features to prove that his personal and political qualities had multiple meanings and a changing character.

THE CHANGES TO HIS HUMAN NATURE THROUGHOUT HIS LIFE

࿐

Just like any other human being, Mandela wasn't a one-dimension persona, and he had more than one identity.

࿐

Some of these identities were remnants of previous personalities which re-emerge from time to time, some coexisted with one another, while some were displaced.

࿐

Example, he wore a Thembu attire in his 1962 court case, where he challenged the jurisdiction of a white magistrate who tried him.

❦

Despite becoming a nationalist and a staunch believer of non-racialism, he never changed his Thembu identity through his life.

❦

He may also have been a communist based on recent evidence. As a lawyer, he found a lot of weight on his identity.

❦

Throughout the various periods of his life, Mandela became a different person. While some of these changes were a result of the conditions he encountered, some of it was his personal choice.

❦

Mandela recalled that he was not born with a "***hunger to be free***" as a young man.

❦

When he was growing up, he had a relatively sheltered existence - he grew up in the home of chief Jongintaba Dalindyebo, the regent of the Thembu people at that time.

❦

Hence, he enjoyed the kind of freedom he desired.

༄༅༅

He only had a confrontation with the racism and the humiliation entailed in apartheid when he arrived in the University of Witwatersrand at the age of 23, any illusions he had of being free was quickly dispelled.

༄༅༅

Despite being influenced by his great mentor, Walter Sisulu and being credited as the co-founder of the ANC youth league, he was reasonably undeveloped as a politician when compared with other leaders such as Ap Mda, Oliver Tambo, Sisulu and Anton Lembede.

༄༅༅

Thus, he had to be guided by Sisulu and Michael Harmel, the communist who gave him a reading list. Then, he dedicated himself entirely to be mentored.

༄༅༅

Since he was known for breaking up meetings of the Indian Congress and communists, he was initially considered to be an extreme Africanist, but by the 1950s, he had become one of the leaders who advanced the cause of multi-racial and non-racial freedom.

MAKING DIFFICULT DECISIONS

✺

Apart from the various forms of struggle which marked the journeys of Mandela's life, he has had to make multiple difficult choices along the way.

✺

While he experienced the various conditions of relative freedom and multiple degrees of constraint, he had to make changes to his decision-making and the actions he took afterward.

✺

He was the first commander of the Mkhonto We Sizwe (MK) to go to prison.

✺

It was while in prison and on a deep meditation when he concluded that the forces of liberation and the apartheid regime are in a stalemate.

✺

The apartheid regime could not suppress the resistance, and at the same time, the forces of liberation were unable to defeat any of the military power it had faced.

✺

Since this presented a situation where negotiations could be the key to resolving the problem, he set about creating the conditions for talks between the apartheid regime and the ANC.

◌⃝⃟

Was this decision entirely his own? Mandela admitted that yes, it was.

◌⃝⃟

Without being given any mandate, he defied the principles of collective decision-making of the ANC.

◌⃝⃟

However, Mandela believed that the opportunity would have been lost if had he not acted when the opportunity presented itself.

◌⃝⃟

This raises two crucial questions:

◌⃝⃟

- Should a leader be allowed to make decisions that can affect his group by himself? Or
- Must a leader consult with his group before making any decision that can affect the group?

◌⃝⃟

Coincidentally, Mandela's interventions were happening at the same time when the leadership in exile were sending feelers to the regime in power. Thus, negotiations were opened and opened up the route to a multi-racial democratic election.

A MIDDLE WAY BETWEEN TWO EXTREMES

༺༻

For some, Mandela compromised the struggle and was a 'sell out,' but for others, he has messianic qualities.

༺༻

Whether or not he was settled is a different discussion entirely, the questions are "***should there or should there never be a compromise in the course of fighting for freedom?***" or "***if there can be a compromise, when can you justify it?***"

༺༻

The truth is, when real political discussions (that involves the loss of lives) are being discussed, there has to be a compromise.

༺༻

Compromises are necessary and can be justified based on three main conditions:

༺༻

When...

⚜

- The cause of freedom can be advanced
- Bloodshed can be reduced
- Peace (one major precondition for liberty) can be attained

⚜

In conclusion, I believe posterity will indicate whether or not he made the right choices and actions either on his own, as part of the ANC or as part of the tripartite alliance leadership collective.

❧ XVI ☙
EPILOGUE

❦

Nelson Mandela remains one of the most inspiring figures in history.

❦

He died at the age of 95 on the 5th of December, 2013.

❦

Here is a summary of why Nelson Mandela continues to be held in high regard even after his death:

❦

Before the legalization of apartheid in South Africa, Nelson

Mandela was one of the few black people to be educated and trained as a lawyer.

❦

As a young man, he witnessed the separate lives being lived by black and white people (who were the minority in the population) when apartheid was legalized in the country. The schools, hospitals, and even beaches made available to the whites had better conditions than those available to black people.

❦

The black population didn't also have access to fundamental rights such as the right to vote or be voted for.

❦

Mandela joined the African national congress (ANC) political party and co-founded the ANC youth league to protest against apartheid since he believed everybody should have equal rights.

❦

Since he as among the leaders of the protests, he was sentenced to life in prison on Robben Island in 1964.

❦

As a prisoner, it was illegal to take his photos or even quote him in public.

❦

Big concerts were held all over the world to campaign for his release.

❦

As president of South Africa in 1990, f.w. De Klerk (a white man) gave Mandela freedom after he had spent 27 years in jail. He received a hero's welcome after his release.

❦

His constant message for forgiveness and equality made him even more famous.

❦

In 1991, apartheid was abolished, and in 1994, the first multi-racial elections were held in South Africa.

❦

Having been elected president, one of Mandela's first tasks was to bring together people from different races in the country.

❦

For his work, he was awarded the Nobel prize for peace in 1993.

❦

The rugby world cup was the first sports competition to be held by South Africa, and this happened during his tenure as president in 1995.

⚜

Though most of South Africa's rugby players were white men, Mandela supported them to unite the country.

⚜

With politicians and celebrities queuing up to take photos with him, he remained one of the world's most famous leaders till his death.

⚜

Though South Africa is still bedeviled by a lot of problems such as disease, violent crimes, and poverty, Nelson Mandela will always be remembered for changing South Africa into a fairer place for its citizens and foreigners.

⚜

His message of peace and unity will continue to be the lasting legacy.

❧ XVII ❧

AFTERWORD

❦

You just discovered more about Nelson Mandela and his legacy.

❦

However, a word of warning – just knowing how to do some something isn't going to give you any result.

❦

That's because the key is that you need to take action on what you just learned.

❦

And that's I encourage you to return to chapter 7 - where we discussed leadership lessons from Nelson Mandela, review the lessons, and then start implementing them right away in your life because you can always practice leadership lessons wherever you maybe regardless of your status.

❦

Because the sooner you do, the sooner you'll start affecting your life and the lives of those around you in a positive manner!

YOUR FREE EBOOK!

As a way of saying thank you for reading our book, we're offering you a free copy of the below eBook.

Happy Reading!

88374869R00080

Made in the USA
Middletown, DE
08 September 2018